Summons

Seasons * Lessons * Prayers
48 Poems

Linda M. Shepard

Goose River Press
Waldoboro, Maine

Copyright © 2020 Linda M. Shepard

All rights reserved. No part of this book may be reproduced in any form without written permission from the publisher, except by a reviewer who may quote brief passages in a review to be printed in a newspaper or magazine.

Library of Congress Card Number: 2019953777

ISBN: 978-1-59713-210-7

First Printing, 2020

Cover photo by Linda M. Shepard.

Published by
Goose River Press
3400 Friendship Road
Waldoboro ME 04572
e-mail: gooseriverpress@roadrunner.com
www.gooseriverpress.com

For John, great blessing in my life.
For Val and Bri, bright lights in my heart.

CONTENTS

SEASONS

Returning//1
Messenger//2
Koan//3
Quiet Light//4
Summer in Winter//5
Maine Mid-October//6
Shoveling Snow as the Half Moon Rises//8
Church//9
April to May//10
Mirror//12
Finch Fan//13
Crossing the Threshold//14
Gloaming//15
Affection of the Moon//16
No Guru Needed//17
Call it a Day//18

LESSONS

Soon//21
The Morning Walk//22
Teacher//24
Winter Dragons//27
She Moves Up From Depression//28
The Changing Sky//29
Flood Waters//30
broken prayer//31

CONTENTS

The Wind Carries the Leaf//32
Departure//33
Maybe I Will//35
Up the Spiral//36
First Child//37
The Fire of Life//38
No Tomorrow//40
angel drops by//42

PRAYERS

Renewal//45
Dream Potion//46
Morning Prayer//47
Love, Still//48
Chisel//49
Toward the Night//51
Lifted//52
Refuge//54
Life Force//55
One Gift//56
Cicada//58
Empty Vessel//60
Her Light//62
Carrying the Pearl//63
Summons//64
Epilogue//65

SEASONS

Returning

The sparks of early spring pull me
out of the house and into the woods.
The air weighted with the smell of life waking up,
I must be there to witness the snow's
final melting
into warming ground
the mist rising and mingling with light and hope.

A scuffle through last November's leaves
reveals fragile blades of pale green.
Small beetles uncovered scatter and burrow.
The raucous ravens take my eyes
to the sky
where they prank and play
in their mysterious bird world.

Tiny winged things have just been born
and fill the air around me.
Wood pecker drums the tree.
The breeze spreads the rich fragrance
of new life and fertility.
Earth regenerating,
life cycles circling around again.

And I, too, another creature ready for rebirth.
Shedding the winter coat, the heavy boots,
scarves and gloves,
feel the sun's heat stirring, firing
gifting me
strength and renewal
as my heart is lifted by the returning light.

Messenger

We are given these moments
unexpected awakenings
when
hiking up the mountain
on a brilliant Sunday morning
marching feet, panting breath, galloping heart,
we stop to drink
and lift our eyes from rocks and roots
the slow brown decay of leaves
oak, beech, birch,
and look out to see the earth
spread before us.
The distant mountains
the shocking blue of blue sky
the clouds skating by high and light laden
the stoic stand of naked trees awaiting
the first winter snow
and the hawk's silent circling
the slow widening spirals
guardian ascending
carries our hearts to peace.

Koan

The ferry pulls away from the dock.
The diesel smoke,
acrid yet comforting
mingles with the salt churned air.

The angled sun
sparkles the expansive sea.
A thousand light tipped waves
carry me to this other shore.

Low tide air,
thick, ancient
redolent with primordial memory,
layered with life and death,
I feel the stirrings of inexplicable joy.

The towering pines spiral upward
intent on their conversations
sky talk, bird talk, wind talk.
Their deep roots anchored and strong,
invisible to me,
yet I feel that earth pull
the downward search
wildly alive, nurtured, sustained.

Craggy rocks, smooth stones
the slowest heartbeat of all,
I listen in giant stillness for their one word
meant for me.

I come to the island to remember.
To remember my face before I was born.

Quiet Light

The winter woods, so different from the summer,
once obscured by clusters of green grasses
leaves and ferns, now exposed and bare.
More beauty for my eyes, the story in the woods.

I see the birch sapling, the small white pine,
moss covered boulders, abandoned bird nests
and a small lacy ice rimmed pond
which no doubt frogs will sing in next spring.

Three forty-five, the air chills with wind.
The sun sags behind the high hill,
the treetops still hold shafts of muted light
but I am cast in shadow.

Like these woods in the oncoming winter
I feel a part of me bare and revealed.
Now the time comes to go inside myself,
down into the darkness and pull forth the light.

Summer in Winter

In deep winter, the sun limps a leap
above the horizon.
Its diffused light foretells the coming storm.
The trees stand in frozen stillness.
The lake, a smooth pewter glaze,
rumbles and groans and thunks
as the ice shifts.

For a while, I depart.

It is the end of a too hot day and
we are floating in the lake
sun still high and bright.
We feel our bodies relax into quiet joy.

Warm wind lifting small waves.
The leaves and reeds move rhythmically.
A loon surfaces and dives,
close enough we see her red eye.
Later, a summer dinner in the gazebo
as evening robin song drifts down from
the heavy-leafed trees.
The good wine a quiet song in our veins.

Later still in bed, windows open
the humid air covers our bodies
like a thin blanket, the pulsing drone
of the crickets lulls us to sleep.

A sudden rattle of window pane startles me.
I open my eyes to see the
predicted snowstorm has arrived,
the wind pushing reality back into my day.

Maine, Mid-October

The intensity of this day
presses on my chest.
The deep stillness, a perfect calm,
the brilliance of the
crystalline blue sky,
cloudless.
How is it that
beauty creates this ache,
a stirring
a deep longing to remember
something I've lost?

A flock of starlings
disbands from a treetop.
Randomly
they drop in silence
down to the big oak
instantly disappearing.
Their movements let loose
the last of the acorns
they click, tick
as they fall through the branches.

Eight geese glide down
and land by the farm pond.
The cows glance at me
with mild interest,
placidly they pull the grass
their jaws working sideways.
I hear their huffing breath.
A sheep bleats somewhere.

My eyes move
to the sunlit red sumac,
sticks of flame
which brighten the woods.
The last purple asters,
bees still busy in them,
bow to the ground
with flower-laden stems.

The trees are on fire again.
How is it
that we are not riveted,
open-jawed and awed,
eyes amazed
by this colorful blaze?

How is it
that the once green leaves,
the earth's lung and breath
transmute their lives
into this silent, beautiful death
releasing the trees to open sky?

Shoveling Snow as the Half Moon Rises

Do you have those moments when
without preface,
without seeking or intention
the world stops for you
and the moment blossoms
opening and expanding
the small aperture of routine and repetition
and suddenly
you see with bright eyes and happy heart
the blessed fullness of your life?
There it is,
in the guise
of the most ordinary moments
like a basket full of sunlit gems
ancient gifts
earthly riches spilled.
You look up to the vast sky.
You are held by
the stillness of the evening,
the silence of the stars.

Church

Three stars are visible in the early evening sky.
A line of geese, black against the cobalt blue,
weaving with random intention,
passes overhead.
I crane my neck to watch.
Eyes open
face to celestial heavens
is how I pray.

There is a holiness,
an unbroken line of poetry
woven into the world of Nature,
this fantastic and mysterious creation
of which we are part.
It is the rhyme of every blossoming spring,
careless of winter's brutal beauty,
arising again with winds, bees, fragrance,
the slow opening tulip and poppy and rose.
It is the rhythm of ocean tides,
sunset arcing to sunrise
season's songs the lyrical flow
of every passing year.
It is the pulsing of breath,
pausing for birth and death.
And we,
strands of light in this Master's weaving,
offer praise
and sing open
the heart of holy.

April to May

And so now,
let us begin the invitation to spring.
Sweep the front step, clean the windows
hang the screens.
Begin the ritual of raking,
check the buds on lilac, magnolia, young peach.
Renew the clothes pins,
tighten the line, hang the sheets.

The heavy quilts get stored,
bring out the bright colored ones,
the shorts and sandals.
We've already noticed with a quiet happiness
how the rising sun
now enters the kitchen window
a new slant, a new intensity.

Sit longer with your coffee, your tea,
your morning ritual.
There are more birds singing now
which must be noted.
Turn the soil and plant the seeds,
letting your face welcome the sun.

This sweet time,
the simple joy as the season begins,
so fragile are the new shoots,
the trees slowly greening,
the air beginning to sway
with the movement of small lives,
the air textured
with the lacy weight of fragrance.

How many more times
will I be granted the privilege
of seeing this miracle?
The answer, for everyone is this:
we cannot know.
And so, my prayer for you and for myself...
may we stay awake to beauty,
may we stay awake with love.

Mirror

Clouds hanging heavy and low today
the darkening afternoon brings a deep quiet
an atmosphere of ease
a visible stillness.

I am a mirror to the mood of this day
no mental agitation
no physical restlessness
no troubled thoughts spinning webs.

The simplicity of being overtakes me.
Looking at the motionless bare trees
a strange and solid contentment
anchors me to this chair.

I cannot awaken ambitions.
Pared down and emptied
I feel my heart in my chest
beating the rhythm of peace.

Finch Fan

The sweet tweet, the flutey song,
feathers fly as they ruffle and fuss at the feeder
casting seeds to the ground
so doves and cardinals join the feast.
There is something about small birds,
wind blown, brave hearts, persistent and cheery.

It's a magician's trick,
a small mystery,
how a dark mood dissipates
like steam from a kettle
by simply stopping,
watching,
to remember again
the easy access to joy in any moment.
To remember again the wild mystery of
this world, this fleeting life
this flash of light
which is me, perfect, whole, welcomed.

Finch, the yellow shaman in the trees,
finch as mantra,
little zen master has struck me on the shoulder:
Wake Up!
This is it.
Now is all there is.

Crossing the Threshold

We feel the light changing as much as we see it.
Our eyes and mind adjusting to the approaching winter.
It seeps into us.

We feel it through the lives of geese gathering
to go elsewhere,
their familiar song, longing, full of memory.

We see it in the pink and purple asters waving
in the chilling breeze.
Acorns patter down, milkweeds fluff and fly.

Apples rotting on the ground have turned brown.
Orb weavers spin in the fields.
A sunrise caught in the cold dewey web shimmers.

The moon looms
large and orange and stars seem brighter, close.
The shadows lengthen, the arc of the sun shifts.

The evocative smell of wood smoke saturates the air.
It is cozy, melancholy, it is fringed with fear.
It says gather, be prepared, settle in, slow down.

It is this,
the cusp of change which has caught our
deeper knowing. We feel the pull to pause.

To acknowledge an ending and a beginning.
To mark the continuity of cycles.
To praise the ceaseless beauty around us.

Gloaming

It is gloaming
and I am roaming
deeper into the darkening woods.
The giant pines
like sacred signs
black silhouettes of great beings
all seeing
guardians to me.
Mesmerized
by the falling snow
my thoughts begin to slow
the rhythm of my steps
a chanter's call
I fall
into the trance
of
calm.

Affection of the Moon

January cold descends
the trees are gripped in ice.
A strong wind sets the house
creaking and snapping.
The weight of the layered quilts
presses me to the cold bed.

A full moon lifts slowly
off the sharp black tree tops
laying its pale light
across the old wooden floor
creeping up over the covers
it finds my face.
The warmth is imagined
but the touch is sweet.

No Guru Needed

A walk in the woods today,
a desire to fill myself with November's calm,
gray sky, brown ground, the old pines' deep green.
Climbing the hill
I am given gifts.
Crow song, a piece of quartz,
a pod I do not recognize,
my pant cuffs burr studded.

I descend emptying.
My thoughts, trailing behind me
dissolve like vapor.
The quiet stream winds beside the path,
a soft song bubbling over smooth stones.
I arrive at the bottom of the hill
a hollowed being.
Dipping my hands in icy water, anointed.

Call it a Day

Late November,
wrapping up some final garden chores,
the air growing chilly and damp.
Let's call it a day.

Inside the warm house now,
I happily kick off my boots and tie up the apron.
Cutting squash,
the sweet full smell of harvest fills my nose.

The dusk is slowly settling down.
I look out my kitchen window,
a view to the lake, calm and reflective,
the last flurry of chickadees feeding at the suet,
food to warm them in some distant tree tonight
where they bed down in cold darkness.

Chopping, peeling, slicing,
the sky is moving through shades of blue,
pink rimmed clouds imperceptibly darken to gray.
I fill the pot, turn on the burner, set it to boil.

Then
the sky holds still,
colors remain for minutes... without change
like a held breath,
a deep earthly pause,
a pulling in of light and energy.
I am its mirror.
Holding still,
until....there,
the last breath of day light
is released.

LESSONS

Soon

My heart feels asleep,
vast and strong
but in a state of hibernation.
Its beat is slow with unbroken rhythm.

What spark of seasonal impulse
will begin its timely thaw?
What movement of moon, shift of stars
will align in rightful order?

When will the hand of spirit
reach through the veil
and startle it to wakefulness?
I am not so much consciously withholding

but rather waiting
with lizard-like stillness and absorption.

I wait.
I dream.
I know the deep knowing.

The shift will wake these resting powers.
The truth and awe of this existence will fill me,
replacing the woody pulp
with fire.

The Morning Walk

I see her every day,
same time mid-morning
but not if it's raining or snowing.
She is overweight,
walks painfully on swollen feet,
ankles like tree trunks, stiff and inflexible.
Her puffy thick hands grip the rolling walker,
a functional machine,
glossy black and bright silver
brake levers and metal basket
for carrying groceries.

It is inadvertent, but I cringe
as I watch her laborious progress,
hips locked rocking
a side to side stride.
I catch my own body contracting.
I know each step hurts her.

My gaze moves from her
to the little white mutt,
curly haired, unleashed,
who walks beside her.
He is maybe one foot high at the shoulder,
two feet long from nose to tail tip
which wags like a stumpy flag
windshield wiper rhythm
happy to be out in the air,
pacing his mistress.

She stops, leans heavily.
I see her heaving breath.
He stops and gazes up at her,
tail keeping the beat of cheer and patience.
She begins to move forward again,
he, too, looks ahead
the slowest trot, chipper bouncy steps.

The contrast of this scene
hits my heart every time.
Companionship, pain, devotion.
This unrelenting urge toward life.
How is it we find our way?
How is it we rise
and move to meet the daylight
carrying our burdens, hopes, losses?
This unbreakable human spirit to carry on.

Teacher

A walk in the local park,
finding a bench sun warmed and vacant,
I sit with intent.
My assignment, an hour of mindfulness,
loving kindness, watching without judgment
the rise and fall of thoughts and feelings.
I, a budding buddha.
Easy I think, craving the stillness, empty mind. Ok.

Moments later, the violent punch of music
hammers from open windows,
a beat up old car slams to a halt in the parking lot.
I glance to see palms pummeling the steering wheel,
a body's convulsive jerking,
keeping time I imagine.
A long minute of this bone beating and
suddenly silence.

A large lumbering body peels out of the car,
his eyes throw a look my way,
he lifts his chin to me, "Hey."
a smoker's gravely voice, soft tissue burned.
Pulling chin to chest, my eyes flat,
I fake a lift of my lips. He lands on a nearby bench.
(Oh, I am deep into it now, my heart
pursed tight like my father's disapproving mouth).

My eyes scan the nape of a tattooed neck
(rose and thorn entwined cross)
and forearm
(a dagger lodged through skull and cross bones),
so he's into crosses, I muse, no contradiction there.
The three silver rings climbing each ear,
the stab of dull metal through eyebrow and cheek,
rattles my body with discomfort.

I cannot see him, but only the uniform of the rebel.
I see too clearly my aversion and resistance.
This ingrown nettle stings me,
how I am blinded by the visual, the visceral.
We sit, I motionless with retraction,
he is sucking smoke while strange
jumping legs vibrate to music I cannot hear.
We are waiting for something.

Minutes later, another car arrives.
He turns, recognition transforms his face.
I see him for a moment,
he is a boy, receiving a present.
Eighteen maybe, he is years younger than
my own grown daughters.
A wisp of a girl, eyes tired but bright,
carries a bundle to him.

He bows his head and encircles both,
his skull and dagger pressing her back,
he speaks to her hair.
Slowly, with cumbersome care
he receives
the yellow blanket and a perfect round head.
The child
is swallowed by his arms.

The girl looks on appraising, pleased.
Familiar sounds rise from the huddle of three,
ancient, universal, imprinting.
A prayer for them,
unexpected and formed,
fills my aching throat:
"Take care, be gentle always,
remember this love."

Winter Dragons

The stars hang bright and cold
you are in the hibernating curl
the meeting of spiral top to spiral bottom.

If you said yes to this inner cave
what would surface to catch your reluctant eye?
Is your sadness like a stone
sunk into the soft spot of your heart?

Your losses locked in a box with tightened lid?
Your fear a scarf circling your throat?
Your rage so red you paint it white?

Can you open the door to these
ghosts of midnight and give them room to rest?
Don't push them away, don't turn your face.
It is in the embrace the healing begins.

The power of your soul, split from its source,
is calling the wise one in you,
the one who has always known.

You were never divided.
You were never alone.
Fragments hold the wholeness.

She Moves Up from Depression

Like a diamond deep in the earth
sustains a force bearing down,
heat builds
compressing blackness
into exquisite perfection.
Facets to catch the light,
to draw it in and cast it out.

Incubation, preparation.
Powers gather around her,
internal birthing pains
form her
break her
until sky beauty earth beauty
call her
blossom her soul into the world's
waiting arms.

Now she,
the vessel,
pours forth her gifts.

The Changing Sky

The alchemy of the journey starts
the day you drop your history.
You look at the fears, you name the feelings,
you sit down in the fire.
Your stories will come and go, come and go.

This life long blossoming, knowing who we are,
is a dance of constant tension.
The uncovering of understanding, the remembering,
only to forget and then to remember again
the true face of grace at the core of our being.

Turning toward the morning you watch
the new light opening the sky of your mind.
Like the dry earth drinks deeply the rain,
sink in.
Like a bee landing in the unfolding rose,
arrive.
Receive yourself into this
brief and beautiful life.

Flood Waters

Moving like flood waters,
we never stop to touch the trees
along the banks,
their deep roots holding fast.
We are swept in the flow too fast
to see the birds
nesting in those trees.
Distracted
by the lure of the imagined future,
we miss the moment.

I would tell you
slow down now,
stand still and listen,
or sit down.

Give up searching.

Watch
how the miracle of life
springs from stillness;
the tightly layered bud,
the mysterious cocoon,
the alchemist's dream,
the daylight bending to dusk,
the empty sky before the storm.

broken prayer

a touch
to the surface of still water
finger dimples the glassy skin
my heart breaks slightly
like the parting of water
to let you in

a look
a small river of new delight
sensitive being
carrying bundled burdens
your eyes full
with what i was seeing

a time
the waters flooded my shores
the overspilling desire
my unspoken words useless
in the presence of
longing and fire

a fate
untouched and unloved
by the waters of you
emptying out what was yours to have
my heart breaks slightly
to let you go through

The Wind Carries the Leaf

The Tao says:
go the easy way.
Rise in the morning
keeping simplicity by your side.
Let the day unfold without pushing.
Meet your tasks with mind relaxed,
heart light,
the future no where to be seen.
No hurries, no worries they say.
This is a choice you could make.

Go the easy way.
Remain unruffled
by surprising turns,
or
ruffle up and raggle and rage,
but be quick about it.
Then return to yourself.

To go the easy way
is to know that the way
is already going.
Lift up your feet
and let the current carry you.
There is a ride to be taken
a path to be strolled.
The blueprint is laid,
so walk the labyrinth with ease
a soft focus,
and abiding trust.
Go the easy way.

Departure

Death crept into the room 3:35 a.m. while
moon sliver thin and white
slid down into the window frame
gentle light cast on his drawn face.

His straining limbs and fear inflamed eyes
powerless in your presence.
Is it you who siphons his spirit away
to an unknown world?

Settling now, the final letting go,
freed from the clinging terror
the fierce resistance and denial
the long slow decline.

Some speak of you like a darkness
swallowing all light, a coldness entering
stealing warmth and movement
draining out the essence we call his life.

But they may have it all wrong
their own fears obscuring a different truth.
Are you just a pulse beat in existence,
the insubstantial space

between one breath and another?
Perhaps he felt your arrival
like a welcomed embrace,
familiar and comforting.

Perhaps you are as gentle
as a passing breeze
a movement in the tops of spring trees
barely disturbing the nesting birds.

Maybe I Will

I'm going on my "I'm So Alone Solo Journey"
is what my dream figure said to me.
He was short and somewhat stout in build
young, maybe 32 big backpack and beard
stubble just beginning.

I told him in my telepathic dream voice
I could never do that feeling the snap
of fear in my belly just as the thought of
it entered my imagination and
he replied in the same wordless dream voice

I think you can. You could.
And so I wake and feel the residue sensation
of the conversation wondering about his
aloneness his solitude his destination
and the thoughts he carries

and the weight and snug fit of his backpack.
I unconsciously shift my shoulders as if
they might be achy or interested in carrying
something different something other than
my current worries and alleged limitations.

Up the Spiral

You call me
your voice shaking I hear the tears.
Your words sorting through the truth of
current emotions upheaved from the past.

You doubt your strength.
I do not hear weakness.
You fear your fear
but I know you.

This is just another layer arising
an unhealed corner of your heart surfacing
and you will do what you
have always done

shine a light on this darkness
sustain your attention investigating
until understanding allows the
gradual unfurling and release

into the breath of freedom
and there you are again,
beautiful, remembered,
whole.

First Child

She laughs and my mind is illumined.
Her gaze reflects the wonder of an
undefined unlimited world.
The perception of her eye draws no lines
harbors no ideas, closes no doors.
She is the innocence and calm
of a still pond
(I drop a pebble)
of fresh snow on a field
(I make footprints)
of a perfect apple hanging from the tree
(I pluck it and take a bite).

The Fire of Life

You have been sitting with your dead mother
for ten hours now.
Her waxen white face slightly blue,
her eyes glued shut, mouth slightly open,
her ice cold hands curled like a talon
you dare not unfold,
her brow soft and unstitched.

Waves of grief and relief
rise and fall rolling through you.
The child in you wakes and you wait
for her eyes to open sleepily,
her chest to lift,
she will cough softly and
ask for water.

You put your hand on her chest again
and feel the strong heat
still radiating from her heart.
This puzzles you, frightens you.
They will come for her in two hours.
You will ask about this
and they will not be able to answer.

You are sure she is dead yet you feel
for a thread of lingering pulse.
You know she is gone.
You have been present for every fading day,
every dose of drug, the cries of pain,
the mysterious visions she spoke to,
the deepening stillness.

You weep and thank her
for the memories you will carry.
You remind her of her goodness
her generosity, her kindness.
You need to hear your own voice
so you speak out loud hoping that
in some parallel world she is hearing you.

They come and gently wrap her,
calling her Mamma, which you do not,
but you understand they are offering
a touch of familiarity and care.
You sign the papers and receive
instruction for cremation and legalities.
The van departs and the emptiness stuns.

It will be months of reviewing in your mind
those final weeks, praying you did all
the right things, that she felt your love.
The strongest memory lingers,
your hand on her hot chest,
the fire of life still burning until
nothing but ashes remain.

No Tomorrow

You can't put it into words
but you know it as a feeling,
a subterranean shift
in your psyche and heart.
You sense it like a flash of movement
in your periphery.
It rises inside you
a subtle unfamiliar new energy.
You feel yourself leaning toward
something.
It is expansive and unnamed.

You hold the course
the comfortable compatibility
with your rhythms and habits
and repetitious routines.
Yet that stirring
that reoccurring spark which
ignites the desire for change
for something new and unknown
continues to fire.
You are frightened and excited
in equal measure.

You know you must do
the thing you most resist.
Welcome it with curiosity
courage, a trust in the journey.
Ask the discerning questions.
Let go of the past, redefine yourself.
Trust the inner compass,
step over the threshold and embrace
the light in your soul
now ready for birth.
There is no tomorrow.

angel drops by

As searchers
we seek
we open passageways deep inside
to where the dark shells break open

and. *there*
is the shaft of light
benign and full of hope
the slow work of myth unfolding

the breath that finally lets go the fear
awakens the wings
and the
grateful stirring of grace.

PRAYERS

Renewal

Great Spirit,
rebirth me fresh.
Paint my brow smooth,
my heart softer.
Pummel out the tension in my body
and mold me to joy.
Leave no part untouched.

Reform me.
Begin again with me.
Wash away the clay of old fears,
pluck out the burrs of impatience,
judgement, doubt.
Fearless and defined,
fling me into the sky of possibility.

Dream Potion

The thrum of the drum
is a stone thrown
into my chest.
Ribs vibrate and breath liberates
its power of sound.
The heart pounds
a beat of its own.
She stomps the ground
she stomps the ground!
Bare feet she turns around.
I hear the cry inside
wakeupwakeupwakeup!
Bells and bangles jangle
her arms and ankles.
She is a wild gypsy
a starlit witch
a laughing dervish
a moon howling child gone wild
with joy.
Her eyes on fire with desire
to break the chain of old pain
her earth song is strong
in her body
she stomps the ground
she stomps the ground!
She is my prayer
wakeupwakeupwakeup!

Morning Prayer

You wake.
Your ears hum with fading sleep,
dreams dissolve under your eyes.
Sweet robin, cardinal and jay, flutey finch
beckon from the sky, the trees.
An embrace of fragrance floats
through your window:
lilac, apple blossom, viburnum, wild rose.

Forget the creaky bones,
the complaining back.
Guard the mind, it will stall, bargain, justify
and steal your day.

Sit up!
Say this prayer:
"I greet the day with love in my heart."
Now, feet to the floor.

Love, Still

This wine, so rich ruby red
this perfect shaped glass
that fits the hand
the wood cracking and popping and
flames pulsing, wood stove comfort.

Dusk leaning in, coming down
this changing of sky
pale blue to cobalt to grey
the quiet shroud embracing us
our silence weightless and warm.

The undercurrent of peace hums
a slow moving river
deep and wide and clear
small eddies of contentment
swirl and circle our hearts.

Like a still life painting
a pause in waking
stopping the wave of time
we are granted this moment,
a familiar ease fills the room.

Looking back we see how
history built today
today creates tomorrow
forty-five years together
and there is love, still.

Chisel

Walking in silence on our late afternoon hike,
we watch sunlight layering through the trees,
shafts wavering. We hear what we've come for.

Solitary, she is invisible in the light bathed
green canopy above us. Hermit thrush, we whisper.
We search for words.

Name it and maybe it can be possessed.
Diaphanous, evaporative, a descending flutter,
a feather falling on a perfect windless moment,

a small handful of confetti let loose,
light pale blue, soft yellow, lady slipper pink.
Droplets of sound that disperse to a mist

before they reach our upturned faces.
We stand motionless to keep her near.
Closing eyes to find understanding:

what strange sweet sadness tightens our throats?
She brushes our hearts, the gentlest touch
like the old hand of the master archeologist

to an imagined treasure.   Tap.   Tap.   Listen.
Evaluating the thickness of stone,
the readiness.   Tap.

Brushing away the dust with care, a holy touch,
like the grandfather's lips to the newborn's
warm temple.   Tap.

There is a story in the stone.
He closes his eyes to see.
Reverence, and the slightest smile shifts his face.

Toward the Night

Dark waters swirl the stars,
blurring my sense of space and ground.
The cold air is a comforting sting in my eyes
my cheeks feel the chill as burn.
I stare at the moving waters,
depth unknown, obstacles unseen.

Stepping into the black expanse like this,
the blind trust and hope
that the prayers I daily tone will be answered
that the unseen gods will bow
to these incessant requests
offering to me the direction I now must go.

Dreams are too watery and vague to trust now.
My thoughts wander in
too many familiar directions
only reinforcing where I am trying
to move away from
and failing to offer up the future's path.

The moon wavers in pieces and never
reunites in these waters, their unceasing
roll and toss toward the sea.
I send off my present self into the light and dark,
journeying toward the new day
when I arrive whole, known, sparked.

Lifted

I wake this morning and there it is,
the veil of anxiety
the dry mouth the tug in the gut
the heart pounding in its cage.
Is it the backlash from an unsettling dream
a hangover from last night's news
the stealth of mortality?
I am untethered. I do not want to be here.

And so the practice begins.
I step outside, 38 degrees
the autumn sun a sharp bright slant.
Every wet leaf
a dazzle of dew and sparkle.
Mist rising from the grass.
Standing still now
I am looking for grounding.

A crow's piercing call startles,
is she talking to me?
A sudden movement from a squirrel
snags my eye. Yes,
winter is coming. Prepare.
Relaxing a little more now
I exhale, my breath is made visible.
I create a story.

Every inhalation is all the love
I have received in my life.
Every exhalation all the love I have given.
I see this ever changing
river of life I am in,
its rolling and lifting and shifting.
Smiling a little more now
I make a decision.

I imagine myself
leaning back into this river.
Arms spread, floating.
I allow myself to trust, to be carried.
Breathing a little more now,
the morning mist and sun's rays
a simple blessing.
I have always been carried.

Refuge

In the light of love
fear falls away.
Do not
fight yourself in this life any more.
Soften,
open
and row your boat
(gently)
down the stream.
Turn to love
not the shadows on the wall.
Remember,
you were meant to be here.

Life Force

The seed rests in holy stillness.
A vast moment
pre-creation
a breath neither coming nor going
but holding both.
The potential,
full and unexpressed
does not hum with impatience
or shimmer with a force urgent for birth.
It simply rests.
Does it know of its destined self
soon to be called into life?
Will ancestral voices encourage its unfolding?
What mysterious force spirals down
from invisible worlds saying
It is Time to Awaken.
Now.

Spirit yearns to see it's own light.
The seed rests in holy stillness.

One Gift

Raised by a loosely Catholic mother
  and a careless father
church was required for a time.

Rituals and smells and words
  and swirling colorful cloth
blur in confusion in my young mind.

The booming voice of stoney Father Flint
  scaring and scarring
little children with devils and hell.

The odd wafer we ate
  nauseating my stomach
we were told was the body of Christ.

The unchanging liturgy
  the repetition repetition repetition
the mantra of hypnosis.

But one gift was given to me:
the figure of Mother Mary
benign, generous
ever available and no price
to pay for her attention.

In my adult mind I carry her now.
I will tell you this secret.
She lives in an ancient stone church
in a remote part of Ireland.
She is ephemeral

until called upon, at which time
she takes form and will stand at
the opened heavy wooden door,
the arched entrance framing her.
She allows no one to enter

but will greet you without words.
She extends her hands to you
cupped as if to hold cooling water
which is her way of saying
she is willing to receive.

So you give her your fear
your grief your hopelessness
your anxiety and soon begin to feel
your heart and throat relaxing
your breath easing.

She is just like you remember
seeing her in books and paintings.
She is the warmth and comfort you
needed in your fevered dreams.
She is the one mother we all cry for.

Cicada

Seventeen years buried
underground the darkness of home.
Then some divine spark says
    dig out
    move toward the light
    find a tree
    climb up
    stay.
    Wait.
Then its back begins to undulate buckle
and exoskeleton splits apart.
    Now climb out of that crack.
    Wait.
While the old skin
translucent paper thin husk glues to the
brown bark of the tree
the new born creature seems to breathe life
into his wings
inflating lengthening forming them
to perfection
as his new body hardens
moved by the
instruction of ancient information.
The wings
beautiful now
flawless design
ready to take flight.

I want *that*.
To see the old psyche
a wisp of form blown away into spring winds.
To open to the new cycle.
I *want* that.
The caul of fear
residue disharmony
old skins of ancestry to
fall away as I emerge
fragile but whole
newly awakened
ready to open **my** wings
my eyes
my heart
welcoming the liberation and
the touch
    of the divine.

Empty Vessel

The avalanche
drops from the face of the mountain
with an unearthly thunder and
a mad river of whiteness is
sweeping everything in its path
tumbling frothing to the bottom
where the sudden silence feels
like a God-filled moment.

The bowl
just out of the kiln sits on the table.
The sun through the window
hits its smooth curve so the
beautiful glaze is now made manifest.
The deep brick red, the autumn sky blue
the spring green like a bud seemingly fragile
yet resilient with its potential beauty.

The rock
is pounded daily by this tidal power.
For ten thousand years the smack and smash
of waves has carved its shape
smoothed its edges entered its cracks
to split and hone new patterns.
Now the waters curl and caress with an effortless
roll and flow around this ancient being.

The past
which has encumbered and splintered me
has fallen away leaving in its wake
a whispered song without words
an open palm with no expectation
a stillness both unknown and familiar.
Our remaining years, an open horizon.
How is that emptiness can feel so full?

Her Light

You are lucky
   if she turns her eyes toward you—
   a moonbeam on a calm lake
   a sun ray shot through clouds.

Your cards are good
   if she brings her attention to you—
   the embrace of a gentle mother
   the care of sisterly love.

You are blessed in life
   if she calls you friend—
   a wide mountain of compassion
   a quiet garden of gifts.

Carrying the Pearl

Deep in the stillness
alive in the joyful light
and the dark pathos,
tangled in the wild fluctuations
of love and fear,
wisdom and ignorance,
the heart shelters the truth.

The essence of all life
is birthed in the breath
of this immense infinite force,
the immutable light cascading
its boundless creations,
desiring to fill the universe with
its one great song.

The ground of our being
is embraced by this radiance.
We can wait a lifetime for its
cocoon shattering emergence
or be awakened by it
in brief illumined moments,
the sacred lifted out of the ordinary.

As connection to source expands
and we wake from the illusional sleep,
the new cycle of humanity
will begin its destined evolution.
The clear light, the infinite light,
the soul's shining jewel will create again
a new heaven on earth.

Summons

Like hungry breath to dying embers
pulls forth the hidden flames
I call God,
      rekindle my light.

Like hieroglyphic etchings of frost
birthed on frozen glass pane
I ask God,
      sketch on my heart.

Like spring breezes tumbling invisible
carrying fragrance and hope
I sing God,
      ease the weight.

Like sunlight's journey through
the diamond's prism
I summon God,
      break open your spectrum through me.

Epilogue

I am an old woman now.
Wrinkled and weathered
I move more slowly
speak more reverently
listen more attentively.

I am a grandmother now.
My children have children
who sit on my lap
tell me their dreams
hold my hands tightly.

I am an old wife now.
They say we look so alike
that we laugh the same way
walk the same step
it's just our friendship.

I am a dying woman now.
Life has been long
my days have been full
and I greet my death
yet my thirst is unquenched.

Linda Shepard lives in a quiet rural town in Maine where she and her husband raised their daughters. Seeking to cultivate a life of service, simplicity and beauty, she has planted beautiful gardens, played with fabric artistry, volunteered with Hospice and taught yoga for many years.

Summons represents a tapestry of the passage of time; the cycles of personal growth, and a reverent distillation of life observed.

www.ingramcontent.com/pod-product-compliance
Lightning Source LLC
Chambersburg PA
CBHW030533080526
44586CB00011B/418